Standardized Education

Standardized Education
Moving America to the Right

Arthur Lieber

Illustrations by Carol Ruzicka

Copyright © 2011 by Arthur H. Lieber

All rights reserved. No part of this publication may be reproduced in any form or by any means without the written permission of the author; except by a reviewer, who may quote brief passages for a review.

arthurlieber07@gmail.com

ISBN: 978-0-9837696-5-1
Library of Congress Control Number: 2011937566

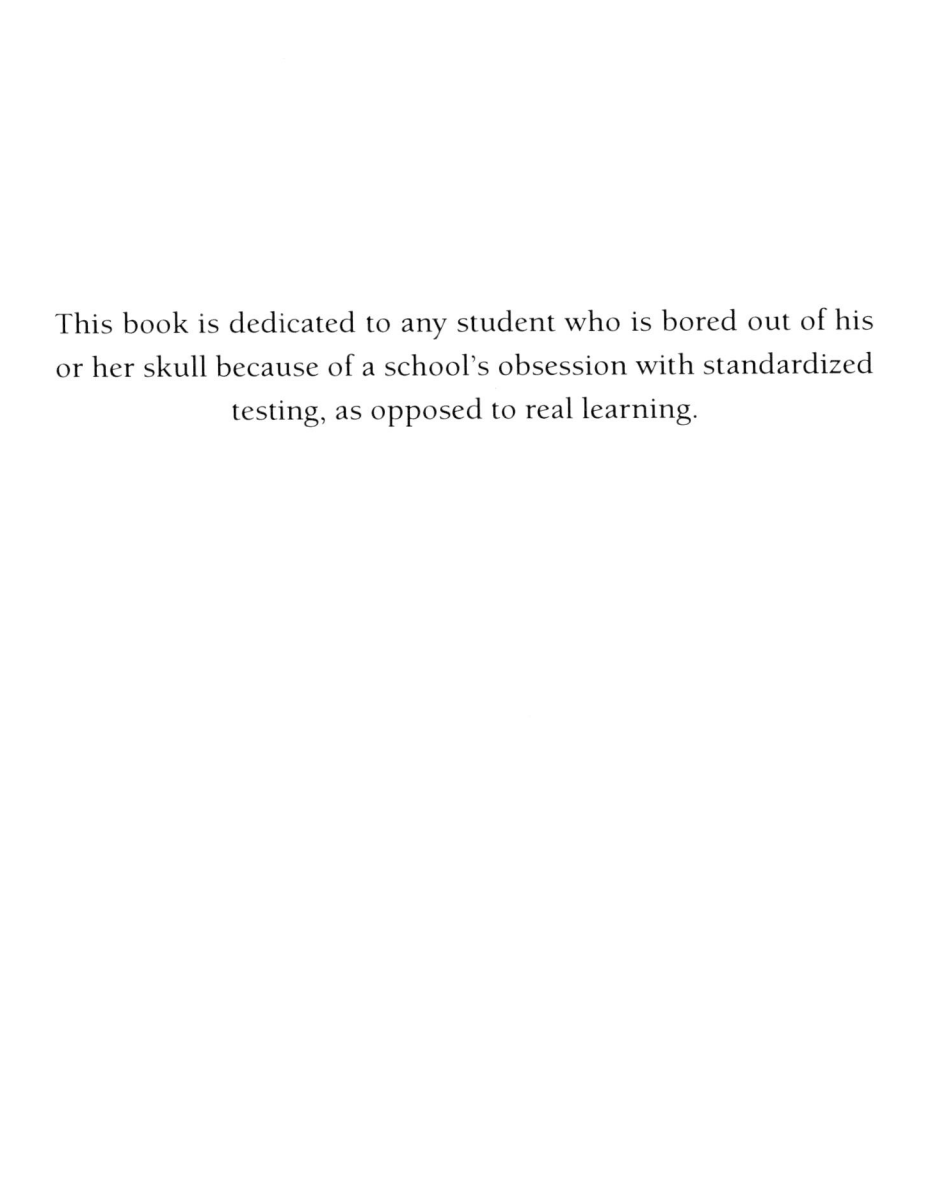

This book is dedicated to any student who is bored out of his or her skull because of a school's obsession with standardized testing, as opposed to real learning.

Contents

Acknowledgments ... ix

Introduction · Education Is an Art, Not a Science ... xiii

Part 1 How Education Fails to Promote a Just and Compassionate Society ... 1

1. The Importance of Empathy in Teaching and Learning ... 3
2. The Necessity of Teaching Critical-Thinking Skills in a Democracy ... 7
3. Did Our Schools Turn Baby Boomers into Conservatives? ... 13
4. Looking for School Improvement in All the Wrong Places ... 19
5. The two "As" of Education: Amnesia and "adultery" ... 25

Part 2 How We Got Where We Are Today ... 33

6. The Transformation of Education after World War II ... 35
7. "A Nation at Risk": Our Education Race with Japan ... 39
8. The Rise of Testing and Competition in Schools ... 43
9. Presumptuous School Names, Bragging Contests, and Enhanced Tracking ... 49
10. Gifted Education: A New Money Making Industry ... 55
11. Schools Run According to Republican Values ... 63

Part 3 Teaching Compassion and Social Justice in
    Our Schools   69

12 Toward an Educational System that Promotes a Just Society 71
13 The News School: a Model for Teaching Active Citizenship 79
14 Wrapping It Up   85
   Notes   87

Acknowledgments

The idea for this book probably started the first day that I was bored in school. I can't remember if that was kindergarten or first grade.

Since then I've had numerous conversations about schools. It didn't take long for me to see a connection between the way in which many of our schools are run and how we have a dysfunctional political system that serves those who least need government.

I thank the many people who have indulged me in talking about the connections between poor schools and poor citizenship. Most particularly I want to thank my wife, Gloria Bilchik, who has challenged my ideas in a supportive fashion and who has helped me refine ideas. She is also an excellent editor.

Thanks also to whomever suggested to me that I post a request for an illustrator on Craig'slist. I reviewed many responses. Carol Ruzicka's e-mail gave me access to her terrific work and also a glimpse into her political thoughts, which seemed to be right in my comfort area—progressive and also on the irony channel. I've never had the benefit of art work in anything I've written. Carol, many thanks for making the book more interesting and also easier to read.

Thanks to those who critiqued the books, most particularly Cori Austin, Bobbi Clemons, Madonna Gauding, Mark Schusky, and Barbara Lindauer. Cori gave me the needed perspective of someone who is currently immersed in both politics and school. Bobbi "figured out" school at an early age and is now a political junkie. Her thoughts are invaluable. Mark and Barbara are rare teachers who see schools through the prism of what is happening in the broader world in which we live. That means they're committed to enriching educational experiences for students but also can laugh at both their foibles and those of others.

Madonna gave the book structure where little existed. She is a remarkable designer and has once again utilized her skills to make a book of mine much more user friendly to the readers. Madonna also kept me focused on the need for progressives to express their thoughts as clearly as possible.

Renee Shur proofread the original manuscript and found a mountain's worth of items that needed clarification, deletion, or addition. Her detailed corrections brought clarity and unity where it did not exist.

Lisa Fox from No Waste Publishing was once again an outstanding publisher with whom to work. Her calm demeanor and knowledge of her business made the final step of producing the book extremely easy.

When I was twenty-six, I was co-founder of what was clearly a progressive school in St. Louis called Crossroads School. So many teachers and students who passed the door brought both joy and insight to me. I am truly excited that students and staff who were at the school in the early years are now in constant communication and will have a reunion in the summer of 2012. If there is any form of evaluation of a school that might be of value, it is what the students who went there are like years after graduation. Even that is subjective, but I hope to get a better sense of what we did well and what we did poorly by getting their adult perspectives on it.

Thanks also to the many students who have participated in programs sponsored by our non-profit, Civitas (Active Citizen 360). You've kept me motivated, given me opportunities to try new ways to interest students, and provided me with many laughs.

Introduction

Education Is an Art, Not a Science

WARNING: Much of what you read in this book will be contrary to the perspectives of professional educators. I take the point of view that the field of education is in many ways more accurately an art form than a science. I will draw conclusions that in many cases are subjective but consistent with the following quote that has been attributed to either Mark Twain, Casey Stengel, or Yogi Berra (all born in Missouri).

> It ain't what you don't know that gets you into trouble. It's what you know for sure that just ain't so.

Coming from any of the three, it would have merit. Coming from all three it's gold.

There are educators who can't accept this level of uncertainty in their chosen field. If they did, much of what they said would not be worth the dollars they are paid to pontificate. Many academic positions in schools of education and educational bureaucracies would have to be eliminated. The reason is that so many people in these positions do not acknowledge the limitations of their knowledge. I have trouble with that as well. That's why I'm inserting this caveat to warn you to be cautious about what you read in this book and to invite you to take exception with my assertions, as well as those of others.

While on the subject of uncertainty, I should mention that much of my experience in education comes from my fifteen years as a teacher and school director at Crossroads School in St. Louis, Missouri. I was twenty-six years old when several of us founded the school. We were all young and committed to providing a combination of traditional academics with a wide range of experiences outside the classroom. In educational parlance, this is called experiential education.

Often times we were asked if we were doing a good job. We were positively assessed by an established accreditation organization, the Independent Schools Association of the Central States. We were the topic of considerable discussion, since we were the sole private, nonsectarian high school in the city of St. Louis.

Were we a good school? Did we as teachers and administrators do a good job? My answer is that it beats the hell out of me. Or to quote Barack Obama in reference to a different topic, "It's above my pay grade."

All I can say is that we were the sum of many different parts. These included how we interacted with students, what we tried to teach, how students responded to what we tried to do, and how students responded to one another.

The impact of much of what we did was invisible to us, the students, the parents, and any professional evaluators. What were students thinking? Were teachers satisfied with what they were doing?

We did have tests and other various forms of evaluation. They gave us slender openings into what was happening in the lives of children. The conclusions we were able to draw were more like hypotheses and hunches as to how to proceed. They were not conclusive like the score of a sporting event where one team wins and the other loses. Presumably there would be more clarity about how effective we were with each group of students several decades after they graduated.

By virtue of the law of averages, we did some things well and we screwed other things up. If I were asked to categorize what went into each of these columns, I'd certainly make some mistakes. On balance, I think that we did well. But it was never at such a level for us or anyone else to crow about.

What happened at Crossroads is not unique. Every school is a mixture of experiences involving a number of people. Some of what happens is visible. Most is not. Just as I will resist the temptation to characterize what we did at Crossroads or what kind of school it was, I will suggest that drawing definitive conclusions about any school, school district, type of school, or education in general is fraught with hazards. In order for this book to have some meaning, I'll make assertions because they help illustrate the dynamics of what is happening. But again, I caution you to read everything with a critical and possibly even skeptical eye.

Invisible is the operative word, because it places limitations on what can and should be measured. If much of what is happening cannot be seen, how can you accurately measure anything of meaning? Education has become a full-fledged social science. The key word is science because it is the ticket to gain and keep your bona fides in the world of academics. It is anathema to professionals to acknowledge that they often cannot see what they want to measure. If that is the case, why are they trying to measure that which can't be accurately measured? The answer is predictable: because they can. They can because they get away with it. They will be able to so long as the public thinks that the numbers that they crunch about students and schools are meaningful.

Part

1

How Education Fails to Promote a Just and Compassionate Society

1
The Importance of Empathy in Teaching and Learning

There is one other item that is important to put on the table before proceeding any further. An underlying theme of much of what I say is the importance of empathy. A clear definition that Webster's Dictionary gives of empathy is "the action of understanding, being aware of, being sensitive to, and vicariously experiencing the feelings, thoughts, and experience of another person." In plainer English, it means being able to put yourself in someone else's shoes.

Empathy is significant in terms of how people regard one another. It also relates to one's political views. Within a school, it is important for students and teachers alike to be able to understand the perspective from which others come. If a student is having a difficult time at home, a teacher with empathy will cut that student some slack. A climate where there is such empathy can make the difference in terms of the student overcoming the hardships of home life.

In politics, empathy can be extended to a group of people who have experienced hardship. The civil rights movement in the United States had the involvement and support of many white people because they were able to empathize with the plight of African-Americans. A legislative body that is supportive of increasing the minimum wage is empathetic because the members understand the hardships of those who are earning less than $14,500 a year. We can safely say that when anyone in our political process has genuine care and concern for those less fortunate, that individual will have a progressive perspective on politics. I am not going to hesitate to acknowledge that the ideas that I propose in this book to improve education have a basis in empathy. This means that they have a progressive political slant. My bottom line is this: Both education and politics will best be improved if policies are based on empathy.

Some may say that I am applying a political bias to education. I am. But such bias exists in all schools, and usually it is a quite conservative one. The bias is conservative at least to the extent that it is designed to conserve the status quo. Our society is currently leaning to the right and will continue to so long as people are anxious about protecting their self-interest at the expense of generosity towards others in greater need. That's one definition of conservatism.

It is best that we understand that, as individuals, we always have biases. It happens whenever we choose to emphasize one thing over another. Bias is reflected in choice of curriculum and what is valued in a particular school. It's not a question of having or not having a bias. It's a realization that all institutions reflect a bias, and we should (a) be aware of that and (b) be thoughtful about the biases of the organizations to which we belong.

Another reason why positive change in schools and in politics are intertwined is the principle of "practice the process." What this means is that if you set standards for others, you have to act that way yourself. It's not enough to say that people should be honest and then for one to act in a dishonest manner. It's not enough for schools to be sensitive to those most in need in the school community but not to others in the broader community in which they are located. If you say that fairness is a value that is important to you, then you have to practice it in both your school and your politics. There is a disconnect when someone says "let's have a fundraiser to help a deserving student deal with a health problem" and then fails to support a national health-care policy that provides the best we can give to everyone.

The psychologist Abraham Maslow talks about a hierarchy of needs. At the top is a phenomenon called self-actualization. It means being able to integrate one's actions with one's beliefs in a way that is sensitive to others. Self-actualization is not situational. You can't say that we are committed to the well-being of the students in our schools but are not committed to the well-being of all citizens in our country—or, in reality, all citizens of the world. We practice politics in our schools. We need to acknowledge it, and we need to bring consistency between how we want students to act in a school and in society at large. For progressives, the key is empathy. For conservatives, it is generally winning, even at the expense of others. There has been much written about promoting win-win solutions. Schools need to practice this strategy and teach it to students.

2

The Necessity of Teaching Critical Thinking Skills in a Democracy

Take a look at the following political commercial.[1] In this race for St. Louis County executive, candidate Bill Corrigan distorts both the record and image of incumbent Charlie Dooley. It is the antithesis of elevating the dialogue in our political process. Is this the best that we can do in asking voters to choose one candidate over another? If so, we're in trouble. And indeed we are in trouble.

We can say with a relatively high degree of certainty that this commercial and others like it are effective. If they weren't, candidates and their hired hands wouldn't run them. If a commercial is false or even misleading, it is still viable so long as the populace is gullible enough to believe it. That's a problem. When a citizenry buys into misinformation, the society is in trouble. It sets itself up to have leaders who either don't have the wisdom or the integrity to determine public policy.

Now consider that students in America spend approximately twelve thousand hours in classrooms from the time they are in kindergarten through their senior year. If a student spends two thousand days in school by the time he or she is eighteen, you would want to think that he or she would be sophisticated enough to not be influenced by such a commercial. The ability to be a good b.s. detector is not measured on standardized tests.

Schools simply are not designed to facilitate the kind of personal growth students need to be sophisticated enough to know when information is misleading. Students are often as

Twelve thoursand hours of high school education, and what have I learned about life?

naïve about advertisements for commercial products as they are about political ads. How many articles of clothing do they purchase because of their brand name rather than the quality of the item?

The societal costs of our schools fixating on standardized tests rather than critical thinking are enormous. Unfortunately, our political leaders at all levels of government are lacking in the sophistication that is needed to know when something is not working. These political leaders ultimately are involved in virtually every facet of how our schools work. They control how schools are funded, what can and cannot be taught, what qualifications are needed for teachers, what obstacles are placed in the way of those who want to teach but are not certified, how long the school year should be, and even how important the school's "Friday Night Lights" is relative to enhanced resources for students with special needs.

The question that both our leaders and our society as a whole must ask is, "What connection do these standardized tests have to developing high-school students who, upon graduation, are capable of thinking critically and compassionately about the problems that face us as a community?" And that "us" is the more than seven billion people living on planet earth.

For whatever reason, our leaders, Democrat and Republican, have been reluctant, even scared, to challenge the power of the Almighty Standardized Test. However, where reality has failed fiction has succeeded. Read and/or watch the following exchange at a teacher workshop as presented on the NBC program "Friday Night Lights," on June 24, 2011.[2]

Citizen Questioner:
Getting back to the issue of standardized testing, what improvements can be made in regard to college admissions?

Lead Educator:
I think that one of the options is that Texas needs a baseline for their standardized test scores and accountability for those

scores. Now we can learn a lot from looking at California's Integrated Accountability System and that has the state academic performance index, and it's also monitoring the federal adequate yearly process and program improvement.

Tammy:
And I would like to add just one thing to that if I could. I feel that we've spent a lot of time today talking about these standardized tests, and I think that we've already acknowledged that the system is failing us, and if we continue to just keep looking at these tests and focusing on these tests, then we will fail our students. Then if we keep pushing those kids towards the ever-important test score, we're pushing them to fail.

Lead Educator:
It seems naïve to presume that these test scores don't exist.

Tammy:
I don't mean to presume that they don't exist, but the students have very different needs and we have a responsibility to see what those needs are and to address them.

Lead Educator:
What would you have us do? Sit down with every student in the state?

Tammy:
Yes, I would.

It's remarkable what we can learn from this 215-word exchange. We gain considerable insight into our values. The scene illustrates the divide between the language of bureaucrats and that of advocates for the well-being of students.

Let's start with the seemingly well-intentioned and harmless question in the clip that is submitted by someone who is either a parent or a journalist. "Getting back to the issue of standardized testing, what improvements can be made in regard to college admissions?"

The citizen is interested in two items: college admissions and standardized tests. It is this kind of question that sets the table for educational bureaucrats to focus on matters that presumably can be measured, but which also may have no relevance to what students need.

What we need are students who have curiosity about learning, who develop critical thinking skills, and who have a commitment to being a positive-change agents in our society. Not only are we not doing that well now, but recent history would indicate that our educational system has been helping facilitate the growth of far too few responsible citizens.

3
Did Our Schools Turn Baby Boomers into Conservatives?

I am of the baby-boomer generation. The first presidential election in which I could vote was 1968. What were my choices? Hubert Humphrey, George Wallace, and Richard Nixon. Nixon won, as he wound up doing four of the five times that he was either the presidential or vice-presidential nominee for the GOP. Many in our generation saw the 1960 election of John F. Kennedy over Richard Nixon as Kennedy had described it, passing "the torch from one generation to another." Perhaps if John Kennedy had not been assassinated, we would have evolved towards a sustained progressive agenda, both domestically and in foreign affairs.

Lyndon Johnson succeeded Kennedy and advanced a domestic agenda that promoted human rights and economic gains for the needy in a fashion almost parallel to Franklin Roosevelt. But Johnson became the face of the Vietnam War, an encounter unlike anything America had ever faced before. Hope was based on lies, and the government repeatedly lied to the American people. If students had been inspired by John Kennedy to be part of a generation that advanced the rights and well-being of all Americans, that dream was shattered as Johnson sent so many off to die for no particular reason. The boomers were becoming known as the "me generation" because so many retreated from political involvement and engaged in hedonistic forms of self-satisfaction.

The body politic, and particularly the boomer generation, was in a state of confusion at the time of the 1968 election, and Nixon snuck through to victory. Even though he ramped up the Vietnam War every bit as much as Johnson and was just as deceitful, he was re-elected in 1972. We could say that America lost in the first two elections in which baby boomers participated. However, baby boomers were still a relatively small portion of the voting public, so Nixon's victories could not be directly pinned on us. However, what was clear was that the boomer generation had become fragmented. If there ever was a common goal of promoting human and economic rights, the desperation of the late sixties and early seventies had made us more concerned about our own personal rights and economic well-being.

From the 1972 election to the 2008 election, the proportion of the electorate who were baby boomers increased. If we had been a generation of "peace, love, and harmony," we would have elected leaders who embraced these values. But in the nine presidential elections since then, a Reagan or a Bush was on the ballot on six occasions and they won five of those times. The seven times our baby-boomer generation elected a Nixon, Reagan, or Bush would indicate that we were not a generation looking for economic fairness at home and diplomacy over warfare in foreign affairs.

If our goal was to have an informed and empathetic electorate, we clearly cannot say that the education system of the 1950s and 1960s produced such citizens. The geneses of the problems that exist today were present sixty years ago. While it's impossible to try to measure to what extent schools were responsible for the development of a far more conservative electorate than might have been expected from baby boomers, schools were definitely a key part of the mixture.

What did America need then in the schools charged with educating baby boomers, and what do we need now? Here are a few suggestions:

- Identify the desire to learn and be curious about how things work as the engine that motivates student learning. In other words, motivation comes from within the student rather than being imposed on him or her.
- Develop critical-thinking skills. This involves learning how to gather relevant facts, determining how they fit together, developing a set of possible conclusions from the evidence, and then deciding with reason which conclusion is most appropriate.
- Develop self-esteem, along with the ability to celebrate the successes of others. This is key because trouble ensues when students are encouraged to elevate themselves through the failure of others. Often times this destructive form of competition is an unstated dynamic in a classroom. This lack of regard for the well-being of others is, regrettably, a key part of the Republican-Darwinian view of politics. There is little empathy for those who are suffering and considerable delight in success when it is at the expense of others.
- Develop global awareness. Establish the valuing of fair partnerships with other countries and look for peaceful solutions to international disputes except in the most extreme of circumstances (see Just War Theory).[3]

Consider what our schools currently value versus what would be most helpful to us, and the rest of the world.

What Schools Value:

- Test scores
- Grades
- School spirit
- Homecoming and Prom
- College admissions
- Aggregate scholarship money

What the World Needs:

- Learning to live together harmoniously in a multicultural world
- Providing economic opportunites for all citizens
- Honesty
- Developing creative thinking and problem-solving skills

There are certain issues related to human rights, race relations, environmental protection, voter engagement, and maintaining peace that were quite important to the greatest generation, as well as to many boomers when they were in their younger years. They formed or strengthened organizations to work on these issues. If you want a barometer for how our commitment to positive social change is waning, talk to remaining members of some of the activist organizations from the 1960s and before. The median age of members of many of these organizations is now well over fifty-five when it was closer to thirty before the Reagan era.

A good example is the United Nations Association. In the U.S., the United Nations Association (U.N.A.) was created in

1946 to provide citizen support for the U.N. Most of the founders were individuals who were involved in the movement to ensure that there was a strong international organization in place following World War II. They wanted the U.N. to be more effective than the League of Nations had been following World War I. The leaders of the U.N.A. did a terrific job while they were in their twenties, their thirties, their forties, their fifties, their sixties, their seventies, and some beyond that. However, chapter after chapter across the country has either seen its membership drastically decline or the chapter has actually folded. The reason is that the founders have not been replaced by young people committed to promoting world peace. The organization desperately needs youthful energy, but young adults are involved in other social organizations or doing all that they can to survive in very difficult economic times.

This is true not just the United Nations Assiciation, but also for the American Civil Liberties Union, the N.A.A.C.P., the Sierra Club and even political party organizations. Obviously the dearth of young members is not entirely the fault of our schools, but they have not done their part to encourage students to be active citizens on key issues, such as world peace, civil liberties, and environmental protection.

4
Looking for School Improvement in All the Wrong Places

Most dialogue about improving our schools looks to cosmetic or even irrelevant solutions. Our schools need fresh teachers working under better conditions and enjoying what they're doing. We rarely discuss that. Rather, we talk about what is the best system: public schools, private schools, charter schools, or a voucher combination. This conversation can become an end in itself and we will lose sight of humanizing our schools, something that can't be measured. If an outside observer saw a classroom in which the teacher was engaging, knowledgeable, clear, and focused, and the students were spirited, cooperative, on-task, and productive, the observer should have no way of knowing whether that classroom was in a public, parochial, private, or charter school. The observer would not know if the particular school was part of a voucher system. The observer also wouldn't know how either students or teachers scored on tests.

Additionally, a happy and productive classroom cannot happen in a vacuum. There are other factors at work, including a child's parent(s), neighborhood, safety, economic resources, and, perhaps most importantly, the intellectual and emotional abilities that the student brings into the classroom. We cannot measure what percentage of a child's performance is a result of parenting or schooling, or friends, or any number of kinds of innate intelligence—none of which can be measured in an absolute sense. Educators will continue to try to measure the relative importance of these variables because it's how they get paid and how they keep their jobs.

There are some variables that are important, and common sense tells us so. Depending on the grade level, the subject being taught, the needs of the student, and the skills of the teacher, there is a tipping point at which class size becomes too large. We need to have the resources to not exceed that number.

The resources that money can buy are clearly important. Any teacher who has taught a laboratory science without lab equipment can tell you that he or she is limited in the exeriences that he or she can provide for students. No pun intended, but you don't have to be a scientist to know that.

In general, the more computers the better; the bigger the library the better; the more athletic fields the better; the more art supplies the better; the greater the resources for drama the better. However, these variables also have tipping points or points at which there are diminishing returns. Does a wealthy school need one and a half computers for every student when other schools may have the equivalent of three per classroom? With so much research available on the Internet, do libraries need to have as many volumes as they did in the past? Can drama provide students with opportunities to learn more about the human condition without having exceptional budgets for costumes or sets?

In many ways, high-school sports are a runaway train. I previously referenced the television program "Friday Night Lights" (based on Buzz Bissinger's actual account of high-school football in Texas). There are high-school teams in Texas that have stadiums that seat twenty thousand fans. Allen High School in suburban Dallas is building a new stadium at a cost of $60 million.[4] That's not $60 million for all the schools in the state or for all the schools in a county. It's for one school. You don't have to be a wizard in math to know that the money used to build the stadium will come from other educational and civic needs. It doesn't seem to matter to the football boosters at Allen High. They will tell you that the biggest and most expensive stadium in the country will improve the students' academic performance. No matter how big a stadium is and how many adornments it has, the bottom line is that students are going to compete against one another, eleven on a side. It will take ten yards to get a first down, and a field goal will be worth three points. You don't need a video scoreboard to figure that out.

Artist's drawing of Allen High School's $60 million sports stadium.

It can be argued in many ways that the system of school athletics that we have now is doing at least as much harm to students as good. While it may be good that students are better trained than those who came before them were, the games have become more fierce and violent. Serious injuries are not declining; they're increasing.

A high-school basketball team often will have a season with more than twenty games scheduled. That increases for teams that advance in the playoffs. Think about the student who is taking five "solid" courses and who may be engaged in other extra-curricular activities. The student may have a job, may be needed for home chores, and he or she has games two nights each school week and another one or two on the weekend. Is there time for a life? Is the student being taught the questionable lesson that the importance of sports trumps everything?

Think about the coach of that basketball team who is driving the team in a van or a yellow school bus to a game at a school that is thirty, maybe fifty, miles away. Basketball is a winter sport, and coaches, who often teach, are asked to drive through the worst of conditions just to get another game in.

A football team used to have one or two coaches. One of the real treats of the occupation was to teach student athletes to be smart on the field. Coaches now want athletes to be smart, but it's very formulaic and didactic. "Here's the play book and here's what you do on each play. Whatever you do, don't deviate from our game plan or whatever plays we send in to you from the sidelines."

Years ago quarterbacks actually ran the offense, and middle linebackers ran the defense. They knew the plays well. They knew the strengths and weaknesses of their teammates. If a wide receiver noticed that a defender was shading him to the inside, he could tell the quarterback who might then call a play in which the receiver went down and then out to the sidelines.

While occasionally plays were called in from the sidelines, in general the thinking was done on the field, and it reflected the preparation done during the week. When the game began, there was a real sense of self-reliance on the part of the players.

Most high-school sports are now very mechanized and much less empowering to students than they used to be. It's almost as if the players are pawns that the coaches impersonally move around. Much of the joy has been taken out of sports, although coaches tend to protect their own vicarious pleasure.

The crowds are bigger, the cheerleading is more complicated, and the whole event is more like a social ritual than a game. The odd thing is how little many of the fans actually know about what's happening on the field. When I've had occasion to ask cheerleaders about the game the night before, more often than not they cannot tell me who won. They're not even sure who their team played.

While competitive sports in high schools has taken a far larger piece of the time pie in high schools, time for physical activities in elementary and some middle schools has been dangerously diminished. We read the figures about increased obesity among our youth, but schools cut back or eliminate recess. Not only does recess provide needed physical activity, it gives students opportunities to participate in sports in ways that are much more natural and age appropriate. Just think of an inexpensive red rubber ball on a playground or in a park. There are a myriad of things that one person or a group can do with it. An imaginative child can create his or her own game. Small or large groups can play games ranging from kickball to dodge ball that involve everyone participating in a democratic fashion. Left to their own devices, kids will either play by the actual rules or create their own rules that are more to their liking.

The story of the movie *Field of Dreams* is not about winning the game. It's about a parent and a child playing a game of catch. No one is yelling at anyone; no one is trying to humiliate anyone else. It's just plain fun physical activity, and it teaches people, young and old, how to engage in collaborative activities with that sense of relaxation and spontaneity that has essentially been diminished in "Friday Night Lights"–type sports.

Just playing is enriching in itself. Additionally, recess is a way for schools to save teachers, administrators, and even politicians from their own devices. When a kid is playing, he or she is neither competing in a highly charged athletic event nor locked into a chair-desk taking the Iowa Tests of Basic Skills. Adults are doing no harm, and kids are growing.

5
The Two "A's" of Education: "Amnesia" and "Adultery"

We tend to complicate education because we can't pinpoint exactly what it is or what it should be. When schools assess themselves, they do not look at what kind of citizens their graduates will be, either at the time of graduation or several decades later. Wouldn't it be important to see how engaged a school's graduates are in trying to promote those values that sustain a just and fair society? If graduates are not involved in trying to promote justice, then the educational system, along with a number of other factors, need to be re-examined. What is clear is that performing well on standardized tests has not produced a nation of responsible citizens.

What both students and society need is education in responsible citizenship. But this goal has been trumped by our fixation with test scores and college admissions.

How did schools become so rigid, so prescribed, and so full of pressure? I think the answer lies in the two 'A's—amnesia and adultery. I'm not talking about the garden variety of either of these phenomena but rather an evolution in how we see (or don't see) schools as our experiences in them as a student becomes more and more distant in our rear-view mirrors, and we move on to other phases of our lives.

By amnesia, I mean teachers, parents, and administrators forgetting what it was like to be a student. They frequently forget how they felt in school when they had (a) unreasonable homework assignments, (b) tests largely unrelated to their subject matter, (c) teachers who were uninspiring, even boring, and (d) teachers who were not particularly knowledgeable in their subject areas. For these reasons and others, school was often a drag for students. When our education leaders were students, how much time did they spend looking at the clock to count down the number of minutes remaining in the class? How often were they passing notes to other students on a subject thoroughly unrelated to what supposedly was going on in the class? How many times were they doodling?

No matter how we change schools, those phenomena will continue. It does not seem mathematically possible for a student to spend ten thousand hours in school and not have moments of boredom or distraction. However, as we move to bring meaningful reform to our schools, first and foremost we need to address this reality and develop programs and techniques that are designed to minimize the cognitive dissidence (drifting off) of students. It amazes me that when educators get together to address improving schools, reforms often involve making schools more boring for students. What can be more of a drag for kids than constantly taking tests?

Actually, there is something: the multitude of classes that schools now offer students in how to take tests. Clearly what these educators are doing is trying to fit students into neat little boxes in which they go through the motions of largely meaningless activities that are a reflection of top-down education designed to satisfy the needs of the educators, not the students.

Often times when I am with teachers and administrators, I try to visualize what they must have been like when they were students. Some clearly would not have tolerated boredom. Others would have been plain squirrelly. The bottom line is that they would have wanted to learn and to have fun learning.

Why are these kids like this? I wasn't like this as a student!

For whatever reason (and I will leave this to psychologists, sociologists, or others who are students of human behavior), when many individuals switch roles from being students to being teachers, they quickly forget how they viewed school when they were students and replace it with a view that is characterized by what I would call "adultery."

This book is not so tantalizing that I'm going to suggest that the problem with schools is that marriage partners are cheating on one another. As referenced in this book, what I mean by adultery has nothing to do with sex and very little to do with loyalty. What it means is acting in a fashion that is unique to adults and only adults. It is not the way in which children normally act.

Perhaps the most damaging behavior that adults exercise with children is to operate as if they, the adults, have infinite knowledge, and the students know very little. The adult becomes the authority figure which is different from being an authoritative figure. The adult often uses authority to oppress students to try to keep them in their place.

However, there is an even more insidious form of adultery that does damage to students, teachers, and schools. It is when adults engage in behavior that includes a great deal of hypocrisy, and that disingenuous behavior is apparent to students. Often times, adults design activities that, for no particular reason, are exclusive to them and exclusionary to students. The problem is compounded when adults indulge in the very kind of behavior for which they demonize students.

For many schools, this form of adultery is most apparent in the special kind of fundraising activities in which "grown-ups" participate. In list form, here is the disconnect:

How Adults Want Students to Behave:

- Do not judge others on superficial criteria
- Be honest, not artificial.
- Treat others equally, regardless of their financial resources.
- Do not pressure others to spend money for something that they may not be able to afford.
- Alcohol and other drugs are bad for you. They distort your thinking in the short run and can have long-term negative consequences.

How Adults Often Behave:

- Engaging in "clothes gaping" and often times making judgments of others based on what they wear.
- Acting artificially because small talk is the currency of the realm, and it would be out of place to engage in serious, meaningful conversation.
- Making an event somewhat exclusionary, out of the financial range of some parents.
- Spending whatever it takes to see and be seen.
- Drinking and being "happy." That's part of the routine, and it's a special privilege reserved for adults.

When I was at Crossroads School, there was a great deal of pressure to have galas and other fundraising events in which parents were the "privileged few," and students were not permitted. I recognized that these events were cash cows and important for a school with serious financial needs, but I did my best to resist such school-sponsored activities. There seemed to be a disconnect between encouraging students to be genuine, real, and sensitive with one another and then going off to an activity that I sponsored and which, for lack of a better term, was quite artificial, even elitist. I don't think that I could have faced the students on Monday morning after having done that. My words about moderation would have rung hollow. Of course, the downside of the approach that I took was that the school passed up opportunities to strengthen its financial position. The pressures I felt in trying to reconcile disconnected activities was one of the reasons I left the school after fifteen years.

*My kids just NAG me for designer clothers regardless of
how much they cost!!*

I am thankful that since my departure others have optimized opportunities for fund-raising for a school operating on a tight budget. If they hadn't, the school would no longer exist. But I could not be a player in the disingenuousness of the fundraising game while trying to encourage integrity among the students.

This is one of the reasons why I think educational vouchers should be given more consideration. This is anathema to many Democrats and often with good reason. However, I think that it's healthy for the educational landscape to constantly be tilled and have new schools created, especially by young teachers. Vouchers could remove many of the financial problems and allow staff to focus on teaching. It's clearly not that simple. As I said previously, the system that we have for schools is less important than the content of what goes on in classrooms and on field trips. As I will discuss in chapter 9, voucher systems, charter schools, and many public schools do everything they can to impress the public by virtue of their names. They also often misrepresent what actually happens in their schools. All of this is counter to the values that presumably we teach students, but that point seems to fly by many educators.

Part

2

How We Got Where We Are Today

6

The Transformation of Education after World War II

To better understand some of the current challenges we face in education, we need to see what happened as we reshaped our educational system after World War II.

Prior to World War II, it was not the norm for every high-school graduate to go to college. Many did not even want to go to college and, instead, preferred the increasing opportunities in well-paying manufacturing jobs. Pay and benefits were improving thanks in large part to the work of active unions. However, part of the American dream following the war was that all children would have the opportunity to matriculate in a public-school system that would, eventually, prepare them to go to college. Of course, in the late 1940s, the idea of "all children" essentially meant white males.

Public schools changed after World War II because the demands of being the world's superpower necessitated new expectations for America's children. After all, each succeeding generation had the task of preserving what the greatest generation had earned. High schools had to be improved, in part, to prepare more students to go to college. As such, they became much more intense and competitive than they had been in earlier times.

Thanks to the G.I. Bill of Rights and a host of other scholarships, college became affordable to a broader portion of the population. Professionals, such as accountants, lawyers, and architects, were in greater demand, and they required college degrees.

As the 1950s turned into the 1960s, President Dwight D. Eisenhower encouraged us to further improve our educational system, particularly in light of the space race, which found the United States in second place after the Russians launched Sputnik in 1957. What Eisenhower and others failed to foresee were the unintended consequences of the accelerated expansion of our educational system. Eisenhower had warned us of the growth of the military-industrial complex but not of a less visible educational complex, which included our public schools, colleges that were eager to expand, textbook companies, and lobbyists who worked on behalf of each of these interests.

Before the 1950s, there had been considerable disparity among high schools. Some had far greater financial resources than others, and they were largely racially homogenous. In 1954, when the U.S. Supreme Court ruled in favor of *Brown v. Board of Education of Topeka,* a mandate was decreed to integrate our schools. This was not easy because many white Americans felt entitled to their choice of schools. The challenges of school integration were not unique to the South. There was enormous resistance in white ethnic neighborhoods in some of America's largest inner-cities in the North. Nowhere was violence greater than in the Charlestown neighborhood of Boston.

The movement for equality is most frequently associated with desegregation. But economics became as much a reason for migration as race. In the late 1950s, millions of Americans moved out of center cities and into new shiny suburbs where new school districts were formed. These districts provided an escape from integration and were endowed with considerable financial resources. This is because they were largely funded by property taxes, and property was more valuable in the suburbs. When the criminal Willie Sutton was asked why he robbed banks, he said, "Because that's where the money is." And when upwardly mobile Americans were asked why they wanted their children to go to suburban schools, it was for the same reason. That was where the money was.

In the late 1950s and early 1960s, public schools were often seen as fitting into one of three categories: wealthy suburban districts that clearly provided great educations; other districts that were "good, just not great," and urban districts that generally were considered to be doing a poor job of educating students. They were the schools from which many students, parents and teachers hoped to escape. Keep in mind that these categories reflected perceptions, not necessarily realty.

All the colleges, particularly the upper-tier ones, wanted bright students, ideally from the wealthy suburban districts. They also continued their traditional strategy of recruiting from top private and parochial schools.

This rather simplistic classification of schools seemed to work for parents, teachers, students, and the colleges. Financial resources were measurable and important. But high schools were categorized additionally by the colleges to which their graduates were admitted. Where were their graduates going to college? There were tiers within tiers. Every school wanted graduates admitted to Ivy League colleges, most particularly to Harvard, Yale, or Princeton. Next, there was a level of schools that may well have been the equal to the Ivy League colleges in terms of education but just did not have the same cachet. They were still highly regarded and included the likes of Stanford, Northwestern, the University of Chicago, Washington University in St. Louis, Vanderbilt, and a host of others.

Since assessments of colleges are in many ways subjective and also specific to particular areas of study, the ranking of colleges became difficult and questionable. Nevertheless, in 1983 the weekly magazine *U.S. News & World Report* published a special issue called "America's Best Colleges." There were many objections to this survey because, as would be the case with any survey of this nature, it was selective in the criteria that it measured. However, the public generally liked it, and the survey was updated two years later and has become an annual publication ever since. It also was a cash cow for *U.S. News & World Report.*

The current popularity and acceptance of the survey is illustrated by data from the 2007 online version of the publication.[6] Within three days of the rankings release, *The U.S. News* website received 10 million page views compared to 500,000 average views in a typical month.

To some, the excitement over the release of the yearly rankings reflects intense interest and curiosity as to how colleges and universities compare to one another. But to others, this classification presents a distorted view and illustrates the desire of Americans to see measurements of information whether or not they are valid and reliable.

7

"A Nation at Risk:" Our Education Race with Japan

The same year that *U.S. News & World Report* came out with its first rankings (1983), President Ronald Reagan's National Commission on Excellence in Education released a report called "A Nation at Risk."[7] Reagan's secretary of education, T. H. Bell, had observed that the United States' educational system was failing to properly prepare students for a competitive workforce. The commission concluded that wide-ranging reform was needed in America's educational system. Among the recommendations was more emphasis on core subjects in high school curricula. The guidelines suggested four years of English, three years of mathematics, three years of science, and three years of social studies. The commission also called upon schools to resist grade inflation. Furthermore, the guidelines asserted that the time students spent in school each day should be expanded to as long as seven hours and recommended adding 20 to 40 school days to the yearly calendar, raising the number to 200 to 220.

In order to understand the motivations of the commission, it's important to keep in mind that in the late 1970s and into the 1980s, the Japanese economy was booming, while the American economy was growing slowly. There was growing recognition and fear that Japan had created an economic

39

engine that was far more robust than that of the United States. The strength of the Japanese economy was evident to all Americans. Japanese cars were selling at a faster rate than American cars. The conventional wisdom (and probably the truth) was that Japan was producing more reliable automobiles with better features and at a price lower than America's Big Three (G.M., Ford, and Chrysler).

When people purchased television sets, the boxes were far less likely to be traditional American brands, such as General Electric, Zenith, or RCA. Instead, the label beneath the screen was Toshiba, or Samsung, or Hitachi. The same was true with other electronics. While America was the country that was ushering in the computer age, more and more work was being outsourced to Japan.

Americans really became scared when Japanese companies began to acquire or merge with American companies. More and more Japanese were buying real estate in the United States. When, in 1989, a Japanese consortium purchased a controlling interest in the RCA Building in Rockefeller Plaza in New York, there were questions about whether Americans could hold on to anything. In 1945, Japan had surrendered to the United States following World War II. Maybe the United States had won the battle instead of the war, as the Japanese economy had become far more productive than that of the United States.

Observers noted that students in Japan spent far more time in school than their American counterparts, and their curriculum was far more demanding. In comparative tests, Japanese students outperformed their American counterparts at virtually every age level. The answer to American leaders was clear. Schools in the United States had to emulate those in Japan, and that is precisely what "A Nation at Risk" recommended.

The Reagan administration was in somewhat of a quandary when responding to the study. The president had acquiesced to his education secretary's desire for a comprehensive study, but Reagan had trouble with federal involvement in schools. He felt that education was the domain of states. Reagan had opposed the establishment of the U.S. Department of Education in the Jimmy Carter administration that preceded him. During the 1980 campaign, Reagan spoke of abolishing the department as part of his war on "waste." But when he took office, the department was up and running, and he was mandated to appoint a secretary. Reagan couldn't nominate someone for secretary of education who would testify before Congress that his goal was to dismantle the department that he was leading. Furthermore, if members of Congress wanted to weigh in on addressing the nation's educational problems, they needed the department.

While most felt that the federal government should play only an ancillary role in education, they saw the federal government as having resources that could enhance the efforts of states. Perhaps most importantly, the problems with education in the United States, as illustrated by its failure to keep up with Japan, spread across the country. Education was clearly a national problem, and the federal government had to do what it could to ramp up America's schools.

At the local level, school districts and individual schools welcomed more federal involvement. They were eager to accept additional resources, and the federal government had goodies for them that they wanted. There were federal programs ranging from accelerated materials for "gifted" students to supplementary materials for those "at risk." Often times, federal money was available to hire additional staff. This was particularly valuable in working with students who were not performing well and who needed special courses or tutoring. And at the local level the federal money did not come with any more strings attached than the state money.

The upshot was that the U.S. Department of Education was going to stay in place. And while it never became a source of large numbers of dollars flowing into the classroom, it did play the role of further studying American education and establishing standards, or benchmarks, that most educators and politicians felt would help raise the performance of American students to that of Japanese students.

8

The Rise of Testing and Competition in Schools

In some ways, a mini perfect storm was developing in education, as two factors emanating from very different geographic areas were about to come together to drastically change the face of education. With the best of intentions to improve schooling for America's children, the forces combined to take much of the education out of schools and put everyone—students, teachers, parents, administrators, state officials, and federal officials—in a pressure pot that seemed to blind them to what was really ailing American education.

The first factor was the setting of standards by the U.S. Department of Education. This was a key component of George W. Bush's No Child Left Behind Act, passed in 2001. Working hand in glove with state departments of education, the federal government made a commitment to establish clear standards for American schools and the students that populate them. In essence, these were goal posts which gave states, districts, and individual schools targets for which to aim.

President Barack Obama and Education Secretary Arne Duncan altered No Child Left Behind with its Race to the Top program initiated in 2009. The Race established new competition among states with the winners receiving more federal assistance.

Much has been written about the Bush and Obama education programs. The programs fall into two basic categories:

1. The testing is focused on how states, school districts, schools, and individual teachers perform. There is no particular emphasis on students. Students are in essence the mules carrying the baggage for the adults who want to look good. Whereas the Elementary and Secondary Education Act passed in 1965 as part of Lyndon Johnson's Great Society focused on providing remedial resources for students and schools in need, the Bush/Obama strategy lacked the human element in favor of number crunching, often with harsh consequences.

   Perhaps no one has better described the downside of testing than actor Matt Damon when speaking at a rally for teachers on July 30, 2011. Damon, whose mother is an educator, said he achieved his success in large part because teachers at the public schools he attended were not forced to focus on "silly test prep" and instead could work to educate.

   "As I look at my life today, the things that I value about myself, my imagination, my love of acting, my passion for writing, my love of learning, my curiosity, came from the way that I was parented and taught," Damon told the teachers.

   "And none of these qualities that I just mentioned, none of these qualities that I prize so deeply, none of these qualities that have brought me so much joy, that have made me so successful professionally, none of these qualities that make me who I am can be tested," he said.

2. The programs encourage cheating, and it has happened. No one needs a PhD in human behavior to understand that when people are under pressure they're more likely to cheat. The cheating occurs at all levels including students and teachers who change students' answers to make themselves and their schools look good. The cheating runs up the ladder to the superintendent's office. Recently, much has been written about teacher cheating in Atlanta, particularly in 2009. However, it has become a nation-wide problem.

Educator Diane Ravitch did a 180° on the philosophy she had held for forty years. She writes about it in her book, *The Death and Life of the Great American School System: How Testing and Choice Are Undermining Education*. She includes a plethora of examples of cheating, most particularly in New York City and San Diego. But there is anecdotal information from all corners of the country.

So long as our educational emphasis is on test scores rather than increasing opportunities for students to learn in ways that are natural to them, we will continue to have cheating. We need to move beyond denying corruption and instead focus on what we can do to provide the best learning opportunities for each individual child.

The U.S. Department of Education may in many ways reflect much of the population's frustration with Washington. What do the bureaucrats do other than meddle? I suppose that some engage in research that may be of some value. However, I think that they would do a much better job if staff members spent half their time teaching in classrooms. Much of the obsession

Wrong answer . . . I'll just erase it and change it to the correct one.

with testing would evaporate if D.O.E. staff had to face the reality of trying to engage students in real learning.

Besides the Bush/Obama top-down competitive strategies, there is increasing demand for excellence in schools at the community level. The three general classifications that existed before (outstanding schools, good schools, and poor schools) no longer satisfy colleges, parents, teachers, students, and the public in general. New constituencies—local government officials and the real-estate market—have become very invested in how one school compares with another. Once schools ramp up their participation in the measurement game, local officials see schools as reflections of their communities and a statement of how they compare with others. At the same time, the real-estate market has begun to factor in the quality of schools in a given area to price homes and commercial business space.

The combined forces of government officials wanting hard data and the eagerness of schools to enter into competition have changed schools as we know them. But there are other forces at work that began to influence the values being taught in schools.

Traditionally, public schools are supposed to be separate from politics and religion. Maintaining a firewall between education and religion is somewhat easier than it is in politics because there are actions that are tipoffs that education and religion are mixing. Fundamentalist Christians have pushed hard for prayer to be legal and acceptable in public schools. Civil libertarians have by and large successfully resisted prayer in schools on the grounds that (a) any prayer tends to be more reflective of one religion rather than another and (b) students (and their parents) may simply not believe in the value of any prayer. People who are either agnostic on religion or atheists do not want prayer in public schools. They feel that history is replete with churches encroaching in the secular world, and they want to make sure that it does not happen in their schools.

On a literal level, schools also maintain separation from politics. School administrators and teachers make an effort to be as bipartisan as possible. If a Democratic candidate or office holder is going to come to school and address students, then the expectation is that a Republican will be next in order to keep balance.

However, in a somewhat subtle fashion, schools influence the values that are important to students. There are two important factors to keep in mind with regard to this phenomenon. First, one of the fundamental roles of schooling from its beginning has been to pass along dominant cultural values from one generation to the next. The second factor is that with the increased emphasis on testing, which includes intense competition as well as extensive importance on image, schools tend to pass along to students values that are more consistent with Republicans than Democrats. In many ways, this was true even before the increased presence of extreme right-wing policies in the G.O.P.

There is a wild card that should be thrown into the equation to see the influence of conservative values, often inculcated in schools, on our body politic. In order to better understand this wild card, we need to first examine what values are most important to schools. Then we'll explore how they impact upon the nature of our political process.

Here are some of the values that are embedded in our adult mainstream culture that are very much a part of our school systems. These are not absolutes. There are exceptions or qualifications to each assertion. However, they have subtle impacts.

- Competition is not only good, it is a key barometer as to a person's value as a human being.
- It always pays off to respect authority, whether deserved or not, because authority figures have ultimate control over your future.
- It's okay to flaunt authority if you can break rules in a subtle fashion and don't get caught (e.g., cheating).
- Image trumps substance. No matter how superficial clothes, make-up, tattoos, or any form of adornment might be, they receive more attention than the content of one's character.

9
Presumptuous School Names, Bragging Contests, and Enhanced Tracking

Another way in which image has become a runaway freight train is in how we name schools and courses that students take in them. It's no longer sufficient to be Taft Middle School. A school needs to have a presumptuous name like Taft Classical Junior Academy. It's the importance of superficial branding.

A phrase that has become current in politics is that you can put lipstick on a pig, but it's still a pig. The danger in adorning the name of something is not that someone tries to dress something up. The danger is that it plays on the huge amount of susceptibility in the public. There are those who honestly believe that when a school changes its name from Frankfurt to Frankfurt College Preparatory School that the school has actually changed.

In reality, the only thing that actually changes is the name above the school door and the stationery that the school uses. If it were that benign, we'd be okay. The problem occurs when enough people in the public believe that the quality of teaching and the totality of experiences at the school actually change. The public has succumbed to what I call "name-flation." While more people may hold the school in high regard, without substantive changes the school is what it's always been. This phenomenon is so important that school districts and the communities they serve in many ways can avoid improving their schools simply by giving existing ones souped-up names which vulnerable or gullible parents and students buy into.

Magnet schools and charter schools are where name-flation is most prevalent.

Classical College Preparatory, Advanced Studies
TAFT ACADEMY
Character Building, Homework-enhanced

Another way in which schools brag about themselves in a distorted fashion has to do with scholarship money offered to their students. About ten years ago, I was at an awards program just before the end of a school year. The principal was very proud of the senior class. There were about fifty students who were about to graduate. She indicated that as a group they had qualified for over $2 million in financial aid from the colleges they would be attending. I did a little math, and that came to over $40,000 per student. That was clearly impossible. In a good year, a more realistic figure might have been a quarter of that amount.

I thought that what I had heard was just an isolated form of boasting from a magnet school that wanted the world to know how outstanding it was. But in the years that have followed, I have repeatedly heard similar claims. The math just doesn't work.

What was happening was what I was suspecting. The schools were aggregating all the scholarship money that had been offered to students from all the schools to which they applied. There were a number of students who applied to up to ten colleges. If on average each of these colleges offered the student $8,000 in financial aid, then the high school could consider that student as having been offered $80,000 in scholarship money. The last $72,000 of that was funny money because it wasn't going to that student. Once the student informed the nine colleges that he or she would not be attending, the previously offered money would be available for other students from other high schools.

It may have been that when the "financial aid-flation" phenomenon started it was innocent enough. College counselors and principals certainly keep track of the offers made to students. Summing all the offers would be an enjoyable thing to do, especially if you like big numbers. But in this case, it's a meaningless number. The temptation to inflate the scholarship money for the senior class to a seven digit number was just too tempting. I wouldn't doubt that since this so-called financial-aid number has become a form of competition among schools that certain school officials are encouraging bright students to apply to as many colleges as possible. I can't help but wonder what the record is for the amount of college financial aid that a high-school student has been offered. I'm not sure who holds it, but I'm pretty certain that he or she is aware of the "accomplishment," as is his or her high school.

School names are not the only item that has been changed. The names of courses have gone through the "branding cycle" as well. I'm not going to even question whether or not there should be different levels of classes for students. Some of these are presumably more challenging for "brighter" students, while others offer more remedial classes for students who struggle. There are valid arguments to fit classes into a hierarchy of performance. However, there also are compelling reasons to not label students as "gifted," "average," or "slow." I would once again say that trying to make a determination as to whether it's preferable to rank classes or try to present them on a level plain is one that educators can argue about, study, draw their own conclusions about. At the end of the day, there will be no definitive answer, because in the famous and eloquently simply words of the character Bobby Simone in the television show "NYPD Blue," "Everything's a situation." That's about as close as I can come to words to live by.

The fact is that in many schools we put students on different tracks. Some are geared for "fast learners," some for "average" students, and others for "slow learners." There was a time when students were tracked, but it was intended to be subtle. I went to a school where each grade had three sections. There was the A section, the B section and the C section. We all knew that those in the A section were presumably the best students. Those in the B section were good but not great, and those in the C' section had better look out because their days at the school might be numbered. These distinctions were rarely discussed by teachers or students; but, as a student, all you had to do was look around and you saw the reality of how the determination was made as to which students were in which sections.

Ultimately, those who excelled in the A section received honors during and at the conclusion of the school year. As time went on, many schools bestowed a group honor upon the brightest students. They were no longer in the A section. They were now in the Honors section. This change seemed rather harmless. It reflected an honest assessment of the top section. It made students in the honors sections as well as their parents feel good, so it caught on rather readily. There were some downsides. First, some students in other sections felt like second-class citizens. As the term *self-esteem* was becoming part of the common lingo, it was recognized that it didn't do anyone any good to feel bad about him- or herself. Second, in some schools, students who were in the honors classes were harassed for being there. Some were seen as four-eyed intellectual geeks. It was as if they had turned their backs on their friends in other tracks. In some cases, these students were bullied. In other cases, they intentionally failed so as not to be segregated from some of their regular friends.

The term *honors* essentially applied to a particular class. A student might be in honors English, honors math, but in regular history and science. While taking an honors class did give special attention to a student, it still did not fully put the student at a level above most of his or her peers.

10

Gifted Education: A New Money Making Industry

As schools scrambled to make their classes appear more demanding and enriching, there was a growth in what came to be known as gifted classes. No sooner were there gifted classes than there were exclusive programs for gifted students. This was an important distinction, because the adjective *gifted* was being used as much to describe a student as a class or program. For some students, the new programs did indeed provide opportunities that had not existed previously. For others it further segregated them from so-called mainstreamed students.

Unlike honors programs, gifted ones had an impact that went beyond both the student and the school which he or she attended. Essentially, gifted education became a new industry. It's as American as apple pie; perhaps as global as oxygen to seek economic gain when it is possible.

The fact that schools were now initiating gifted programs provided new opportunities for the "university-workshop-credentials" complex to profit. Colleges began to offer new classes, even programs in gifted education. That was definitely a ker-ching for them. More classes meant more revenue. Teachers who previously had taught regular or honors classes were now teachers in gifted programs. Universities created and offered special programs to provide more professional development for teachers who wanted to instruct gifted students. Education bureaucrats who certified teachers also liked university development programs because it gave them something else to assess. In other words, it gave them more reason to justify the existence of their positions and often locked in those positions for the future.

Advanced Placement (A.P.) tests have been around for some time, but recent years have brought what I call A.P.-flation. Initially, the idea of A.P. tests was to give select students opportunities to take classes that presumably would be comparable to classes they would take in college. At the end of the course, students would take tests, graded from 1 (lowest) to 5 (highest). Depending on the score they received on the exam, they would receive varying degrees of college credit.

What gives A.P. classes a certain level of validity is that each class has a uniform curriculum that is used in all schools in which the class is taught. Teachers and students are expected to rigidly follow the curriculum. Barring the very real variable of the quality and style of teachers, students from across the nation take the test having had equal opportunity to learn and study for the material on the test.

The initial idea of A.P. classes was a sound one and somewhat altruistic on the part of colleges. Students could receive college credit without having to take and pay full tuition for them at the colleges. A.P. classes gave some students a real jump starts on completing their undergraduate work in three rather than four years (although summer classes were often involved).

One problem with A.P. classes is that in order to ensure maximum uniformity, they are designed so that one size fits all. Regardless of the learning style of a student or what the student really wanted to learn in the subject area, A.P. courses all cover essentially the same material in essentially the same fashion. It is very mechanistic and has a certain similarity to a factory producing uniform products.

A surprising and unexpected result of A.P. classes for some students is that the uniformity has the impact of teaching students to change their writing styles so that they lose much of their natural written communication skills in order to produce as the program would requires. More than once I have asked seniors and juniors if they would be interested in writing newspaper articles for various publications about projects in which they have participated as part of the work of our educational nonprofit organization (Civitas). The students have told me that they really don't know how to write in a journalistic style. In fact, the only way they know how to write is A.P. style.

The growth of A.P. classes opened even greater economic opportunities for schools and education sycophants. For years there had been programs in which for a significant fee students could study for their College Board tests. These programs had enormous influence on schools because they placed pressure on schools to supplant existing courses with new ones on test taking. Where previously a student might have read novels in which he or she was interested or taken an elective course in art history, the student was now in a test-taking class learning how to best game the system in order to score well on the College Boards.

The growth of A.P. classes has resulted in the expansion of the range of test-prep classes that are taught both inside and outside of schools. Those taught in the schools often mean that more meaningful and engaging classes are either removed from the curriculum or no longer available to students taking A.P. classes. Those taught outside of school give substantial advantages to students who have the resources and the time to take them. These classes are often expensive, beyond the financial range of many students. Furthermore, students who are involved in a variety of extracurricular activities simply do not have time to take these test-prep classes. Students who have outside paying jobs, either by necessity or choice, find it difficult to take advantage of the A.P. option. So while the goal of many organizers and supporters of A.P. tests is to create a level playing field for students, such is not the case because not all students have similar opportunities.

There has been an evolution of the classes that students on the academic fast track can take. At first it was the likes of being in the A section, meaning that more material was covered, often in an accelerated fashion. The classes were designed to challenge the students and give them opportunities to use their academic inclinations to learn more.

Next came the honors classes, which were essentially the same as being in the A section only with a more prestigious title. The next stage in the evolution of unique classes for students who were deemed to be among the brightest was the creation of classes for so-called gifted students. Initially the gifted classes were on an ad hoc basis, offered for certain students in certain subject areas. Then gifted programs were expanded to become a totally separate track in which students took accelerated classes across the board.

Advanced Placement programs began to provide opportunities for students to earn college credit before high-school graduation. However, almost every department in schools wanted to offer A.P. courses. This was in part so that the teachers and the departments in which they taught could maintain the same status as other departments that already had A.P. classes.

The classes that were being offered in many ways reflected Adam Smith's view of capitalism, in which the forces of supply and demand determine the quantity of something and its price.

The students who take advanced classes often have a natural inclination to compete. Given an opportunity to advance their standing, they generally take it. Such became the case with A.P. tests. When they were established, each class was considered to be a prize plum. A student who had an opportunity to take one was considered fortunate. Even if a school offered A.P. classes in a number of disciplines, the general rule was that a student could take only one A.P. class. The reasons were sound. First, the schools wanted to give opportunities to as many students as possible to take the A.P. classes. If you were good in English but for one reason or another you couldn't get in an A.P. English class, then if you were good in science you could apply to take another course, such as A.P. Biology. Second, the schools often felt that the pressures of taking even one A.P. class were so intense that it would be detrimental to a students' overall studies, grade point average, and perhaps even personal well-being if he or she took more than one A.P. class.

These barriers to A.P.-flation have long since been knocked down by the demand of students to have even more demanding course loads and the desire of various departments in high schools to participate in the A.P. program. Not too many years ago, I was surprised to hear of students taking three A.P. exams. Now I hear of some who are in A.P. classes in five subjects of their core curriculum (English, math, social studies, science, and foreign language).

What is the significance of this AP-flation? A lot and a little. Students who take a number of A.P. classes are affected in one or many of the following ways:

- They may be learning more.
- They are under more pressure.
- They compete with one another to take the toughest load further increasing the pressure they experience.
- They can impress others simply by listing the courses that they are taking.
- Their lives are more limited and scripted. Much of the time they are living in an A.P. bubble.
- They move further away from the lives of other students in their schools, as well as students who took accelerated classes prior to enormous growth of A.P. classes.

However, with all the hoopla about A.P. tests, a key question is rarely asked. Are the students learning more than what their predecessors learned who were in the A sections of their classes that did not have embellished course titles? Has the balance between the substance of the courses that students take and the image attached to taking such courses tilted more towards favoring image and less on content? As I have previously stated, there are risks, even hazards, in trying to measure outcomes in education. So I will resist the temptation to say that the A.P. curriculum that many students take today is any better or worse than the A section curriculum that was offered several decades ago.

What we do know is that education is much more complicated than it used to be. Taking classes used to mean taking classes in school. Classes are now offered by a number of outside institutions, often for-profit corporations. Classes now have embellished titles. Honors are bestowed upon students in greater numbers than they used to be.

*So, what do you like to do with your free tiume after your
Advanced Placement courses?*

So what do we have to show for students taking more embellished and so-called accelerated classes? Again, I caution you to question any conclusions I offer.

- We have a generation of students who are better standardized test takers than students of previous era.
- We have trained a generation of students to become quite competent at following directions that come from teachers.
- More students have learned to write in a prescribed style that fits within the guidelines of A.P. courses.
- We have trained a generation of teachers to accept top-down curricula and teach those curricula to students.
- A much greater proportion of a student's education is measured than was the case in previous decades and "the measurement" is accessible to students, teachers, parents, and schools that students may attend in the future, including colleges.

11

Schools Run According to Republican Values

There is a remarkable similarity between how our schools are run, what they value, and what is important to the Republican party. Let's examine some of them.

Conservative:

Schools	Republican Party
Schools accept the dominant culture in America.	The Republican Party wants to maintain the status quo with regard to who has power and who doesn't.

Competitive:

Schools	Republican Party
From pre-school through high school, students are challenged with an ongoing series of standardized tests. They are assessed by how well they do relative to their their peers	The Republican party values competition because it represents survival of the fittest. Of course the competition doesn't begin on a level playing field since Republicans have the advantage of either being wealthy or representing the dominant culture.

Compassionate:

Schools	Republican Party
There is very little compassion or empathy for those who struggle in our schools. They are often told that they are failures because they don't excel as other students do. Those who are least capable of taking care of themselves are often bullied and humiliated	The Republican Party has virtually no compassion or empathy for those among us who suffer. They fight against comprehensive health care, minimum wages, on-going unemployment insurance, and a host of other programs that serve as the safety net for those in need.

But is this what we want in our schools? When we have multiple wars going on against Muslim countries. When we have a lingering 9% unemployment rate. When we have a higher figure for under-employment. When our balance of trade continues to be unbalanced, in favor of imports over exports?

I hope Jane does really poorly on the test.

How can I make my colleague look really bad?

We pass health-care reform, which indeed will provide coverage for more people who desperately need it. But we structure it with a mandate in which individuals buy health insurance from for-profit companies. Thus we make health care an obligation rather than a natural right. Social Security is a right, and it works. We fail to create a health security system that treats citizens with the dignity that they deserve. It would also be cost-saving because no insurance company would be skimming profits off the top.

Over the past thirty years the wealth of the top 10% of Americans has risen over 40%, while it has essentially remained the same for the rest of us. Our environment, which has been threatened by so many pollutants, gained protection from the Environmental Protection Agency and public sentiment at large.

Key to changes over the past thirty years is how money has become so entangled in politics. Following Watergate in the early 1970s, Congress passed caps on how much money candidates could raise and spend. A modicum of sanity was brought to our political process.

However, the U.S. Supreme Court ruled that contributions were a form of free speech and that Congress could curtail them in only a limited fashion. When John McCain was a maverick, he joined with Wisconsin Senator Russ Feingold to once again place limits on contributions. As a bipartisan measure, the legislation passed Congress. However, provisions were chipped away by further legislation and rulings by the courts. Eventually, in the Citizens United case of 2010, McCain–Feingold was essentially gutted.

Even if we had an electorate of individuals schooled in the dynamics of active citizenship, they would have a difficult time determining which candidates to support and which to oppose when so much money was spent to influence them. However, the key is that educated active citizens would instinctively know there is something unfair with the huge amounts of money in politics which is not only large but distributed in a most unfair system.

A better-informed electorate would mean that we could risk trying to change the Constitution where it needs it. Our focus would not be on peripheral and clearly discriminatory measures, like prayer in public schools. Rather it might be on special protection for elections so that the free speech that is protected in the First Amendment could be shaped in such a way as to give an equal playing field to all candidates. We already make exceptions to the First Amendment, including the most notable, which is you can't yell "fire" in a crowded theater. Why can't we say that no candidate can raise and/or spend more than "x" number of dollars?

One of the anomalies of this situation is that liberals are often the individuals who succeed the most in our schools. There is a considerable body of evidence that substantiates that liberals are both more intelligent (a very subjective term) and better educated than conservatives. The "best and the brightest" of our high-school students go to colleges and universities that have traditionally been considered to be among our most liberal.

Often times these individuals have liberal or progressive political views while in high school, when in college, and following graduation. A key tenet of the liberal agenda has been support for our schools. It is somewhat the norm for the children of parents who are progressive and who have succeeded in school to follow in their parents' footsteps. They perform well throughout their school careers, are accepted to and attend our so-called top universities, and sustain the liberal views that their parents have held.

The schools they attend serve them well, in large part because their parents and often their friends embrace the compassion and empathy which is at the root of progressive politics. They learn a great deal in these schools and are strong enough to survive, even flourish with the competition. Like their conservative brethren, they appreciate and take pride in the honors they receive. As they transition from schools to other stages of their lives, they have generally positive feelings about school. They recognize that schools do not serve everyone well and one of the planks in their liberal platform is to improve our schools.

That generally means allocating more money for schools, and supporting programs that provide additional services for both the brightest of our students as well as the most challenged. These programs do not magically occur. They are often designed and implemented by people in university schools of education as well as education bureaucracies at various levels of government. Thus, in a somewhat inadvertent way, they perpetuate and even strengthen the very forces that (a) left many children behind and (b) created the overlap between the values most respected both in our schools and in the Republican party.

One of the biggest obstacles to reforming schools has been the lockstep way in which Democrats and others on the left have attempted to improve schools over the past generation or two. We have the paradox of schools embracing and promulgating Republican values while many of the programs that accomplish this are the brainchildren of and strongly supported by Democrats.

The first step in reforming our schools is a very difficult one. It requires the very liberals who have succeeded in our schools as they are presently constructed to recognize that, in a systemic sense, the schools are producing a nation of more conservatives than liberals. The significance of this is not that Democrats are more likely to lose political races. It is that the empathy that is the basis of the liberal agenda is largely missing in many of our graduates.

Part

3

Teaching Compassion and Social Justice in Our Schools

12

Toward an Educational System that Promotes a Just Society

It is very difficult for us to see ourselves as not generous and kind. We are often called upon to provide charity. It is remarkable how well we respond to a tsunami in Indonesia, an earthquake in Haiti, a hurricane in Louisiana, an earthquake and tsunami in Japan, or a tornado in Joplin, Missouri. Often times those who can least afford to give are among the leaders in providing for others.

Charity is based on the best of intentions and is a natural and, indeed, empathetic response when others are suffering. However, it also tends to blind us to the areas of suffering that are not seen as emergencies. We allow entrenched poverty, the absence of health care, hunger, and homelessness to exist with little effort made to combat them.

The reason is that while we are a charitable nation, we are not necessarily one that believes in justice. The phrase "All men are created equal" at the beginning of the Declaration of Independence is largely forgotten when it comes to income disparity in our nation. Yet it is fundamental to justice, a force that goes well beyond charity.

The signers did not mean that all people should be equally wealthy. They meant that all should have as close as possible to equal opportunities. While we have not, and probably never could, achieve this goal, we have made genuine efforts with the New Deal, the Great Society, and rulings by the Earl Warren Court in the 1950s and 1960s.

A commitment to charity can be incidental; a commitment to justice becomes an engrained value that is practiced every day. Individuals who give to charity often want publicity, ranging from the "here-today-gone-tomorrow" story in the newspaper, to a permanent plaque or engraved stone on a wall that honors their philanthropy.

If a person needs the services of a food pantry, he or she could ask the managers of the pantry for a list of donors. The recipient could admire the names on the list and theoretically write a thank you note to each of them.

However, an individual who is receiving food stamps or living in government-subsidized Section 8 housing would have no individual to thank. The generosity of the government programs for those in need is as significant as the generosity of those who give to charity. However, recipients of government programs are served not because a limited number of people are committed to a particular cause. They receive services because the nation as a whole has entered into a social compact to care for those who, for whatever reason, cannot care for themselves at a given point in time.

For the American dream to mean that every individual who is willing to help him or herself is able to receive opportunities to do so, we must believe in the social compact that John Locke and others described. Most Americans have some familiarity with the Bill of Rights, particularly when any one of those rights applies to a situation in which they find themselves. But few know of the Economic Bill of Rights that President Franklin Roosevelt enunciated in 1944 as the Great Depression was coming to an end and America would be triumphant in the two theaters in which it fought in World War II. A central question that we can ask ourselves about our schools is simply this: Do we want our students to have the often-fleeting knowledge to score well on standardized tests, or do we want them to graduate from high school with a commitment to being part of a social contract that includes the following rights suggested by FDR:[8] He said:

> In our day these economic truths have become accepted as self-evident. We have accepted, so to speak, a second Bill of Rights under which a new basis of security and prosperity can be established for all—regardless of station, race, or creed. Among these are:
>
> The right to a useful and remunerative job in the industries or shops or farms or mines of the nation;
>
> The right to earn enough to provide adequate food and clothing and recreation;
>
> The right of every farmer to raise and sell his products at a return which will give him and his family a decent living;
>
> The right of every businessman, large and small, to trade in an atmosphere of freedom from unfair competition and domination by monopolies at home or abroad;
>
> The right of every family to a decent home;
>
> The right to adequate medical care and the opportunity to achieve and enjoy good health;

The right to adequate protection from the economic fears of old age, sickness, accident, and unemployment;

The right to a good education.

In an era when the rich are getting richer and the poor are struggling more, there are many Americans, particularly but not exclusively Republicans, who would view FDR's proposed rights as a declaration of class warfare. The fact that most high-school students cannot see these rights as both fair and essential is an indication that students are not graduating with a commitment to being an active citizen. They graduate into a culture in which the term *class warfare* is associated with attacks on the wealthy rather than on the poor. So long as students from modest or poor homes graduate and do not see themselves as not having fair access to the American dream, then we have problems. Similarly, so long as wealthy students feel that their rights are being abrogated by less-privileged individuals, then we too have a problem.

So what is needed to change our schools so that they serve a purpose of helping us create generation after generation of active and compassionate citizens?

1. We need to refine our definitions of what it takes to be a good teacher.
    a. It should include:
        - compassion for students.
        - firmness when necessary, so long as it is exercised in a fair manner.
        - knowledge in the subject area that one is teaching.
        - the ability to communicate well with students.
        - a sense of humor (whenever possible).

b. Being a good teacher should not include:
- course requirements in college.
- certification

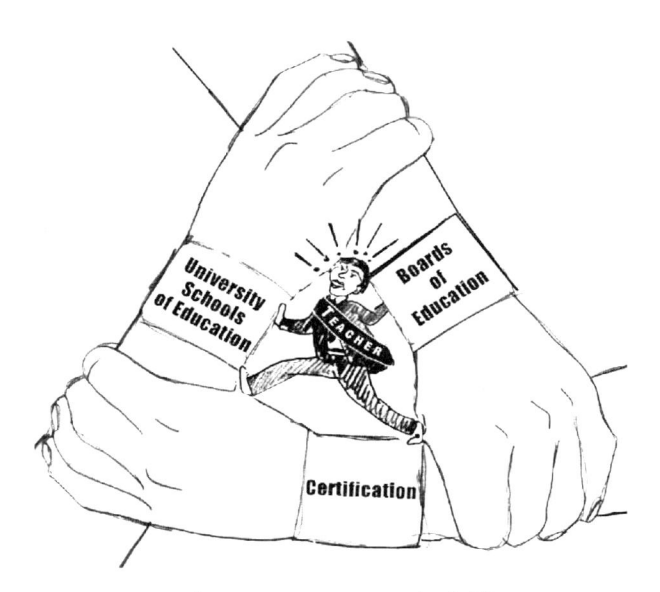

I want my autonomy back!!!

2. We need to pay our teachers far more money. As outlined in my book, *An Unlikely Candidate,* there are numerous ways in which to provide this money. First and foremost savings that can come from implementing a single-payer (Medicare-for-all) health-care system—in which case the jobs of nearly a half million individuals in the health insurance business would no longer be needed. This money could be allocated to enlarging and enriching those in the teaching profession.

3. We should not be exclusionary about the places from which we recruit teachers. Many may not have a degree in education; many may be many years removed from

college. However, if they have life experience that provides key skills for teaching, we should make the door as open for them as for anyone else.

4. A great tip-off for finding good young teachers is to look for individuals who have been camp counselors. They learn a great deal about how to work with students; when they need encouragement; when they need firm guidelines; when they're B.S.-ing; when they're calling out for help. Camps are not nearly as pedagogically driven as schools so former counselors will know how to rely much more on their common sense, which will serve them well in the classroom.

5. We need to recognize that full-time teaching as it is known now is really a time-and-a-half job. Teachers generally work with students from 8:30 AM to 3:30 PM. After that, they spend considerable time grading papers and preparing lessons for the next day. We should change the normal school day of a teacher to one in which he or she teaches half days and spends the other half grading, planning, and, perhaps most importantly, meeting individually with students.

    Another option is part-time teaching and part-time work in other professions. Frequently, this could be in a field related to what an individual teaches, although at times the teacher may prefer to get away from it.

6. We need to get students out of classrooms and into the world around them.

The way it often is . . .

. . . and the way it could be.

13.
The News School: A Model for Teaching Active Citizenship

One of the key reasons why students have so little knowledge about what's happening in the world is that the study of contemporary affairs is essentially shunned by school administrations. It may be that studying the here and now is just too frightening for educators or simply that current events have never had much cache in curricula.

We cannot make progress in helping students develop into responsible and active citizens if they spend very little time studying what is currently happening in the world.

This point was made very clear to me in May 2011 when Osama bin Laden was killed. Like most every other American, I felt a sense of relief. However, I did not find the death of bin Laden to be something to cheer about. Yet no sooner had the news of his death been announced than hundreds of students gathered on Pennsylvania Avenue outside the White House to celebrate and wave flags indicating their joy over his death.

I had written a blog post suggesting that there were many students who did not know much about Osama bin Laden as they were cheering his death. Rather than reacting only by celebrating, I suggested that it might be beneficial for the students if teachers took advantage of the occurrence to make it a teachable moment.

What do I mean by teachable moment? There are times when events occur and are front and center on our radar screen. Before long, they will fade away and possibly be forgotten. The teachable moment requires "seizing the moment."

Keep in mind that when bin Laden was killed, some of the college students who were cheering had very little memory of why he was painted as "the boogie man." They were as young as seven years old when 9/11 occurred.

When American Navy Seals successfully attacked bin Laden's compound, it gave us reason to reflect upon what had happened the previous ten years. Many adults needed to be reminded of past history. Many students needed to learn it for the first time.

Why did 9/11 happen? What grievances did bin Laden and his cohorts have with the United States? Why would they carry out such a horrendous act? How did they get away with it? Why didn't American intelligence learn of it in advance and foil the plot before it ever happened?

Did 9/11 represent a religious war? Did it reflect a cultural war? What about an economic war? Was there any previous history between bin Laden, Al Qaeda, and the United States?

Why did the United States enter Afghanistan shortly after 9/11 to try to hunt down bin Laden? Why did they not find him? How did Iraq get into the picture? Did Saddam Hussein have anything to do with 9/11?

There were so many questions to ask, most with unclear answers. What could the United States and the rest of the world learn from the death of bin Laden and all components of the conflict between Al Qaeda and the Western world?

I was asked to do several radio interviews on why I thought bin Laden's death was a teachable moment in which students could be challenged to do more than shout and wave banners. I did my best to describe how I thought the event provided a unique opportunity to study something of enormous importance. The more we knew, the better equipped we would be to plan wisely for the future.

I was asked frequently if I thought that teachers would indeed try to make it a teachable moment. My response was that regrettably, I rather doubted it. First, many teachers are frightened to talk about anything that might be controversial. Second, many teachers don't even follow the news. Third, many teachers are cogs in the wheel of the so-called teacher-proof curriculum that has been developed by universities, research centers, and publishers. Their job is to cover the material that is forced upon them from above and to not deviate from it.

So on Monday, May 3, the day after bin Laden's death, most teachers proceeded with what they would have done even if bin Laden had not been killed. If they were supposed to have students read pages 326-334 in the textbook and then answer ten questions at the end of the chapter, that's what they would have students do. If it was an American history class, perhaps the material would be about the Federal Reserve system or the Berlin air lift. These are important items and I would suggest that students learn about them, but not necessarily in a sequence that leaves no room for what's happening now.

I ended most of the interviews on a semi-optimistic note, concluding that perhaps students might learn something about the death of bin Laden in some future year like 2014, because by that time there would be updated textbooks that might include some information on what happened in May 2011. Then again, I wasn't sure because how often does a history class ever finish the book and get up to the present?

This is why I am very interested in an idea for teaching history, and potentially other subjects, in a way that is essentially the opposite of how we teach them now. It would be teaching history backwards. Schools would start with the present and then study anything relevant from the past and how that relates to the present situation.

As an example, students would learn about America's current presence in Afghanistan, how it developed over the past ten years, or the past thirty years. Then they would learn more about Afghanistan including its culture, religion, and socio/economic dynamics. Perhaps most importantly, they would learn that no foreign power has successfully conquered what is now Afghanistan since Alexander the Great of Macedon conquered it some twenty-three hundred years ago.

Students could look at economic problems facing America and compare them to the Great Depression as well as a whole series of other recessions and panics that have occurred throughout our history. What solutions seemed to have worked and what didn't? What is Keynesian economics and how would it be applied to today's problem? What is supply-side economics and how would it apply? Is there significance to the fact that the distribution of income in 2011 is very similar to that of 1929? What is the proper role of government in managing the economy? What are the upsides of regulations and what are the downsides? How does the nation's debt relate to household debt? What are the differences between government borrowing and family borrowing? These are just a few of the questions that provide students with opportunities to better understand what is currently happening, often using historical precedent as a guide to possible solutions.

What would this so-called News School look like? Imagine

students coming into a classroom and looking at the day's morning news by whatever digital or print medium might be best. Suppose that a real-estate developer announced plans to redevelop a struggling area but could only do so if he or she could use the power of eminent domain. What is eminent domain? Who sets the standards for it? What does it mean for an area to be blighted? What rights do individuals have when either corporations or governmental entities want to purchase their land at a price determined by a court rather than the market? What happens to how homeowners maintain their property once they hear that it may be seized through eminent domain?

In a News School, you could address all these questions. You could go on field trips to the neighborhoods and ask questions of the residents. You could meet with the developer and ask him or her to respond to your queries.

I have had the pleasure of doing this a number of times with students. It's amazing how much they learn by taking the abstract and experiencing it on the streets of their community or in corporate offices. Students develop the skills to ask pertinent questions. They build the fortitude to actually ask these questions to "official people."

It's not enough to prepare students to become responsible active citizens in the future. There's no reason why they can't be responsible active citizens while they are students. There are a myriad of issues that want for their attention. Adults need to see students at work in all corners of their community. Students need more experiences learning to relate to adults who aren't their parents or teachers. Experiential education focusing on active citizenship would go a long way towards improving both our schools and our political process.

14

Wrapping it Up

When Dan Rather was anchoring the CBS Evening News, he concluded his broadcasts with "and that's part of our world tonight." Each of us sees only a part of the world. Even the media, which wants us to believe that they have an omniscient view of what's happening, see only a small slice of what's happening.

To whatever extent possible, it is desirable to broaden the horizons and perspectives of students. Most of schools now "narrow-cast." They present students with the most restricted views of what the world is about. One of the reasons why I oppose year-round schooling is because regardless of how good a school might be, students need extended periods of time away from the institutions that, left to their own devices, will try to monopolize the students' time. Kids need time to experience the world without "helicopter schools" always hovering around them. Free time is essential. Structured summer programs can also be helpful, but students need to have adult leadership from a different cast of characters than the ones who day in and day out populate their schools.

The more varied and enriching a student's experiences are the more likely he or she is to become sensitive to the needs of others. We can't have the kind of narrow perspective expressed by House Majority Leader Eric Cantor who, following the devastating May 2011 tornado in Joplin, Missouri said that he would only approve aid if money was taken away from another social program. In other words, he wanted to help one group of people but only by punishing a different group.

Our planet has finite resources; and as population grows and we are brought closer and closer together, it becomes more imperative for us to learn how to collaborate with one another for the general good. Students go to school more than two thousand days in grades K through 12. Where better to try to promote respect for others and a sense of shared responsibility for the well-being of our world than in schools?

None of what I propose will come quickly. However, there are many fine teachers working to enrich the lives of students. Our motto need not be the Chinese proverb, "A journey of a thousand miles begins with a single step." We have taken that first step and many more. We just need to engage in reality checks as to the direction of our journey. Presently, our schools seem to be taking us into a world in which key values are very similar to the cold-hearted ones of the Republican party. Many among us are committed to both humane education and a peaceful world. We need to harness our resources and rededicate ourselves to helping each and every child reach his or her full potential. If we do so, we will live in a much more fair and just world.

Notes

1. http://bit.ly/mPy9NU (political commerical)

2. http://bit.ly/osVN4R (Friday Night Lights)

3. http://bit.ly/rrIvDW (just war theory)

4. http://bit.ly/j4uk1v (Football stadium)

5. Fortunately, in the past seventy years the gateway to higher education has broadened to make women and minorities not only welcome but also desired.

6. http://bit.ly/oiuba8 (US news report)

7. http://bit.ly/9Gs9bO (A nation at risk)

8. http://bit.ly/dvXxkN (youtube video)